YOUR GOD-GIVEN DIGNITY

"I loved Jacqui Biernat's Book! From the beautiful, personal photographs and timeless quotes from authors and Scripture - to the insights, actions and challenges for each day, Jacqui's hopeful book about our God-given dignity is a gift! Anyone who picks up this book will be inspired to go through her 30-day process to claim back our God-given dignity and respect and believe God's promises and love. The awesome format, which includes a page to take notes on how God speaks to your heart through her words, encourages the reader to apply what they've read. Let Jacqui's tender approach touch your heart and change your life as she walks beside you on this journey towards new respect for yourself!"

—**Ann Van De Water**, Certified Leadership Parenting Coach and Christian author of *MOMMY MEMOIRS: A Hilarious and Heartwarming Look at the Trials and Triumphs of Being a Mom.*

"Jacqui Biernat has spent much of her life as a coach; encouraging and motivating thousands of people to lead more fulfilling lives. In *Your God Given Dignity*, she combines personal experiences and Scriptural motivation with practical, day-to-day wisdom. With each chapter you'll see that the life you desire *is* attainable. If you have a dream, believe in it. Reach for it! You can make it happen and it starts with this amazing book."

—**Cecil Van Houten**, Family Life Network Radio talk show host, author of *Chasing the Divine*, musician, husband, father and grandfather, Seeker of Truth.

"Through Jacqui and her message, you will feel God's presence, her ability to inspire with genuine light and a beautiful heart of serene encouragement. *Your God-Given Dignity* is rich and profound. It will strengthen your spiritual roots and help you manifest your own radiance."

—**Marcia Wieder** , CEO and Founder of Dream University ®, named 'America's Dream Coach' and 'The Passion Expert' by Oprah Winfrey, is a top rated keynote speaker, a member of The Transformational Leadership Council, and best-selling author of 14 books.

YOUR
GOD-GIVEN
DIGNITY

GIVE YOURSELF THE RESPECT YOU DESERVE—
THE RESPECT GOD GIVES YOU

Jacqui Biernat

NEW YORK

YOUR GOD-GIVEN DIGNITY

GIVE YOURSELF THE RESPECT YOU DESERVE—THE RESPECT GOD GIVES YOU

Published in New York, New York, by Morgan James Publishing. Morgan James and The Entrepreneurial Publisher are trademarks of Morgan James, LLC. www.MorganJamesPublishing.com

The Morgan James Speakers Group can bring authors to your live event. For more information or to book an event visit The Morgan James Speakers Group at www.TheMorganJamesSpeakersGroup.com.

For more information about the author and to sign up to receive her blog posts, visit http://www.YourGodGivenDignity.com

The pictures in this book were taken by family members, with the exception of the cover photos, where noted.

Unless otherwise noted, all Scripture quotations are taken from the King James Version of the Bible.

Scripture quotations marked NKJV are taken from taken from the New King James Version. Copyright © 1982 by Thomas Nelson, Inc. Used by permission. All rights reserved.

A **free** eBook edition is available with the purchase of this print book.

ISBN 978-1-63047-279-5 paperback
ISBN 978-1-63047-280-1 eBook
ISBN 978-1-63047-281-8 hardcover
Library of Congress Control Number: 2014940816

CLEARLY PRINT YOUR NAME ABOVE IN UPPER CASE

Instructions to claim your free eBook edition:
1. Download the BitLit app for Android or iOS
2. Write your name in **UPPER CASE** on the line
3. Use the BitLit app to submit a photo
4. Download your eBook to any device

Cover Design by:
Chris Treccani
www.3dogdesign.net

Interior Design by:
Bonnie Bushman
bonnie@caboodlegraphics.com

In an effort to support local communities, raise awareness and funds, Morgan James Publishing donates a percentage of all book sales for the life of each book to Habitat for Humanity Peninsula and Greater Williamsburg.

Get involved today, visit
www.MorganJamesBuilds.com.

Habitat for Humanity®
Peninsula and
Greater Williamsburg
Building Partner

THERE

Dedication

I am dedicating this book to my husband, Ed, who has loved and believed in me, literally through thick and thin.

I am also giving a special mention to my mother, Connie Foster, who is also a best friend and guide.

My children, Christin, Jeremy, Andrew, and Lydia, also deserve special mention, as they continue to amaze me.

Contents

Foreword

Many authors have written self-help books, both Christian and secular. But few have developed their work through introspection, biblical research, and dedicated daily personal effort. Jacqui Biernat has produced this work through resolve and an exceptional work ethic. Jacqui's dedication and sincerity remind me of the wonderful Edgar A. Guest poem "I'd Rather See a Sermon than Hear One any Day." Specifically the second line reads: "I'd rather one should walk with me than merely tell the way." Not only has Jacqui developed the tenets found in this book while on her personal journey, she continues to utilize them as she develops and nurtures her relationship with God, family, and others.

The title of this book no doubt piqued your interest, for who among us doesn't desire dignity? Well, you have found the perfect guidance, a simple method to establish in your heart of hearts that almighty God loves you. You will learn He yearns for you to embrace the self-respect and dignity that are justifiably yours. This will result in a blessed lifestyle awakening from the realization that God has chosen you to be His child. You will see that learning to love yourself will vastly improve your capacity to love God as well as your fellow man.

If you have longed to change your life, get ready because change is on the horizon! This book is packed with inspirational quotes, relevant Scripture, and a practical routine designed to be easily entreated and simply put into use.

Contained in these pages you will find objective building for obtainable goals, with frequent challenges and reminders to be thankful. This work is, simply put, a do-it-together kit—that is, you and God putting your life into an order that you and He are happy with.

If being a whole person—fit physically and emotionally—appeals to you, rejoice, because you have found a great start. We are where we are in life because of the choices and decisions we have made. If we choose correctly, we can expect results. Choosing this work will produce results if results are what you are after. But then, aren't we all?

This book is not about theological anthropology or manmade religion. It is from the perspective of a family relationship. While there is much religion in Christianity, true Christianity is not about what men do. It is about a loving Father and His family.

You may have read other self-help books which touted Christianity, but I assure you none are like this one. This is about you being a whole person unquestionably convinced that God loves you, and you in turn will learn to love yourself.

Who better to guide and teach you than a proven faithful wife and mother? Jacqui is such a woman. I'm reminded of the verse: "Who can find a virtuous woman? For her price [is] far above rubies" (Proverbs 31:10 AV).

Herein you will find keys to developing healthy biblical self-esteem. Not only will you become fit physically but you will also replace years of disappointing misery and depression with joy and a satisfied mind.

As it is written in Isaiah 61:3b, "…to give unto them beauty for ashes, the oil of joy for mourning, the garment of praise for the spirit of heaviness…."

Your God-Given Dignity will show you how to begin that life-altering pilgrimage.

—Rev. Linus A. Mathis III
Founder and director of Frontier Christian Ministries Inc.
Publisher and editor of "On the Frontier"
Author of *God's Desire Regarding Healing* and *The Good Hope*

Introduction:

Giving Hope

The definition of insanity is doing the same thing in the same way and expecting different results.
—Attributed to an ancient Chinese proverb, Ben Franklin, Albert Einstein, and Rita Mae Browne

We know that we should not repeat the same actions if we want things in our lives to change. And yet, we seem to be creatures of habit, falling into routines and thought patterns that are often detrimental. We tell ourselves that's just the way I am.

However, we see others change, get inspired by that, and try doing the same but fail yet again. We wonder, what is their secret? Why can they get it done? What's wrong with me?

Nothing is wrong with us. It isn't a secret. It's a learnable skill and process. We can also get it done with understanding and application of the same principles that successful people use. There really are keys to success. There is nothing new under the sun; the principles are as old as time and spelled out in one of the oldest texts in the world, the Bible.

In this book, I use biblical texts and quotes from other sources, as well as pictures, to highlight these principles and the thirty days of giving yourself the respect and then the love that you deserve.

Understanding Why

I put this together for a reason. I want to help and bless you because I've been on this path a while myself. The pictures used were taken by my husband, other family members, or me, and they are very special to me. I wanted to include them because our minds work best with pictures or symbols to help us remember. I'm still on the path, and I know there are some who are far ahead of me. I'm not one of the speediest on this path, either. I'd love to have you walk with me, though. We can adjust the speed because it's not important.

It's a joyful lifetime walk, having the peace of God in our hearts, His joy in our minds and bodies, and His love to give. When you have a good case of a cold, others can catch it. When you truly understand God's love for you, you can respect and love yourself, and then you can give a hefty dose of that love to others. Acting on the self-respect manifests itself in our lives as dignity.

Understanding What

The basic premise of this book is to acknowledge that we have the freedom to choose, and that God gave the gift of free will to us. We need to understand what it is that we have and how to use it. The back story: For all of humankind, God formed our bodies, and made us in His image and likeness (love, light), in our minds and souls. Within the first man, He created spirit life to easily communicate with Him. The first of mankind, Adam and Eve, were three-part beings: body, soul, and spirit. God wanted a family and relationship with humankind so He could do what He does best—love. He also gave us free will to control our own thoughts and decide our own path.

Certainly God understands the workings of the universe and of humankind and expected a certain level of trust. Adam chose a different path and did the opposite of what God had asked, then lied about it. God had said ahead of time that if Adam went against God, he would die. Adam didn't physically die, but the spiritual connection that he'd had with God disappeared. It took the "second Adam," Jesus Christ, to pay the price with his life, to regain that full spiritual connection with God for us.

> *For whom he did foreknow, he also did predestinate to be conformed to the image of his Son, that he might be the firstborn among many brethren.*
> —Romans 8:29

(The Old Testament prophets had the Spirit upon them, not within them, and it was conditional upon their being in obedience to God; whereas, we can now have the Spirit within, and it is unconditional and permanent.) Because we as humankind are made in God's image of love and light, we can be our best selves when we remember the sacrifice, and that the verse above refers to us as the many brethren. We can exhibit these traits to the world and be a force for good. The spiritual connection is our source, our strength, and our gift. What we have a good case of, we can give. God first loved us, so much so that He gave us His Son. As a parent myself, I cannot begin to estimate that degree of love. We have been given the privilege to love others.

Again, it is our minds that determine what we will do. We decide.

In the past ten years, the study of positive psychology, epigenetics, neurolinguistics, and other mind research has revealed to us more about the workings of the mind than in the past one hundred years. This research dispels the theory that genes control our lives. The nature-versus-nurture debate has been around for a long time. It has now been proven that it is not nature that is our predominant controlling mechanism. It is nurture. The cells in our bodies respond and change according to signals that they receive from the environment, filtered through our own individual receptors, which have their own interpretation or perception—not all of which is accurate, but we determine what is accurate for us.

Understanding How

What we are today is based on the input we have received in our lives and the filter that we observe the world through. Everyone has a filter—a worldview, perspective, or opinion based on the values acquired from ages zero to seven—and that is how we make our decisions.

> *And be not conformed to this world; but be ye transformed by the renewing of your mind, that ye may prove what is that good, and acceptable and perfect, will of God.*
> —Romans 12:2

In Romans 12:2, God tells us to renew our minds and the fabulous result of doing so. We have power over our thoughts. We can stop them from running wild. We don't have to track according to the negatives we hear in the media and other places. We can put ourselves on an entirely different track.

> *And have put on the new man, which is renewed in knowledge after the image of Him that created him.*
> —Colossians 3:10

In Colossians, we are directed to put on new thoughts according to what we learn from God's Word about the love and light of God. In other words, our minds don't automatically change when we obtain His spirit within us. We are encouraged to do the work by obtaining the knowledge and holding it in our brains. That is why we can still make errors in judgment and sometimes in heart even though we are spiritual people. That is why there is forgiveness. We have to train our minds to obey us. It takes time and practice, but it is doable. We have habit patterns and beliefs that need to be put in alignment with God's Word, His love letter to us.

When our minds are in alignment with God, we have great joy, peace, and abundant blessings. It is also referred to as being in fellowship with God. It is a relationship with God, who loves us. We recognize and live in awareness and thankfulness of these blessings. We tell our minds that the blessings are true, regardless of whether or not they are seen in our lives presently. The best blessings are the ones that money cannot buy, like health, family harmony, a good night's sleep, and a peaceful heart.

We trust first, then see. We believe first, then see. What we say has to correspond with what we trust and believe. The more we trust God, the more peace we have in our lives, knowing that He is for us and is always with us. As individuals, we practice daily mindfulness—a renewed mind, a new mind in harmony with God. When we practice daily mindfulness (a renewed mind) by putting it into practice in our lives, we begin to build self-trust, then self-respect and love.

The quality of being worthy of love is dignity. With Christ's sacrifice, we have been made worthy. It becomes an upward spiral, when too often the way of the world is a downward one. I need you. You need me. We need each other. We need to see that light and love through our relationships with God and one another.

In this book and online, I will give you exercises and mindful activities to begin this journey. Have fun with it. You can do it in thirty days or establish habits over a longer period, say thirty weeks. If possible, do this together with a friend or small group and share the experience. It will help everyone stay on track and will keep it enjoyable.

You can use this guide over and over again, as each time you will be in a new place mentally and spiritually.

When you sign up online, I will send you a daily reminder to help your new practices. When you practice, you will begin to strengthen your mind muscle (that is, renewing your mind) to be in closer alignment to the way you really wish to be.

My prayer for you is that you enjoy the journey, acknowledge yourself for any and all progress you make, and refrain from criticism or judgment of yourself when (notice I didn't say *if*) you don't do everything. In doing so, my prayer is that you reclaim more of the personal light that has already been given to you, and His joy. I want to see you begin your upward spiral—and I would love to hear about it! This book is meant to be the beginning of an awakening to new possibilities, new mindfulness, and other practices that you can continue to use to enhance your journey in this life with God.

In Christ's love,

Jacqui Biernat

Sign up for the online support!

http://www.YourGodGivenDignity.com

Day 1

Day 1 Quotes:

But seek ye first the kingdom of God, and his righteousness; and all these things shall be added unto you.
　　　　—Matthew 6:33

And in the morning, rising up a great while before day, he went out, and departed into a solitary place, and there prayed.
　　　　—Mark 1:35

Insight:

God would have us seek Him first and foremost in our minds and hearts—a very special place reserved for Him. If it was important for Jesus to rise up early and pray, as perfectly in alignment with God as he was, then it is also important for us. There are reasons for success. This is one. It is something that I wish I had figured out how to make more time for when I was young. The peace of mind that comes from this practice carries throughout the day.

Remember that you can carve out a moment here and there to pray, take a deep breath, and still your mind to actually hear from God, no matter what time of day. He is always there for you. Take a moment right now to place your feet flat on the floor, sit up, close your eyes, and take a slow, deep breath in and out several times. I feel better already. How about you?

Actions to Take for Day 1:

1. This may very well be the most difficult thing that I ask you to do: remember that God loves you, and therefore, you love yourself. Tell yourself out loud while looking in your eyes in a mirror, "I love you. God loves you." It is necessary to say in order to convince yourself. Stick with it every day as you go through this book—at least once a day. You get bonus points for doing it more!

2. Take some quiet time to figure out what you want to accomplish this next month while going through these pages: increased faithfulness to finish something; a certain amount of personal quiet, meditation, or prayer time; connections with important people in your life, etc. It can be a big dream or a small one. What is your dream or goal? Whatever it is for you, write it down (there are blank pages at the end of each day just for this purpose).

Make sure it's reasonable for this time period and that you will know when it is completed by having some kind of measurement: if you make a chart, it's more likely that you'll stick with it and be rewarded when you see it filled in. (There's one on my website for you!) That's one way to measure. Make sure you see it as a positive measure of reward and not a negative measure of lack. We are looking for progress, not perfection. Give yourself the same respect you would give a friend. Be your own friend. Love yourself the way God does.

Challenge for Today:

Tell someone else your dream. It will help by holding you accountable. They might ask how it's going!

Day 2

Day 2 Quotes:

Joy is not in things; it is in us.
—Richard Wagner

For this day is holy unto our Lord: neither be ye sorry; for the joy of the Lord is your strength.
—Nehemiah 8:10

Insight:

Who can resist a smiling baby? I sure can't—especially when it's my grandchild! If you really look in that little face, you will see her pure self and all the joy that's resident there. I encourage you to soak it in and really feel the bubbly, free laughter. Give yourself a treat.

I especially cannot resist laughing and smiling because this one is my first grandchild, the one that made it possible for me to be a grandma. This is a role that I more deeply cherish as more grandchildren are added. If you have that in your life, you are truly blessed as well. Children giggle and smile often. When was the last time you giggled? Try doing something really silly, and free yourself to feel that bubbly, effervescent giddiness that's in a giggle. Lighten up!

The quotes above remind us that our greatest joy comes from the depths of our hearts—our priorities in relationships, the first being our quiet relationship with God. God is our source of joy. Feel it. He loves us.

Really! Understanding that He loves us is the first step in loving ourselves. Joy in life most often comes from the things that cannot be purchased with money. They come from relationships nurtured and doing what you love. Giggling enhances your quality of life. You can feel joy in a giggle!

Actions to Take for Day 2:

1. Say out loud while looking in the mirror, "I love you. God loves you."

2. Keep reading out loud your one-month dream or goal from Day 1. Even if you do just these two things for the rest of the month, your life will change.

3. Think through your life so far and write down a list of three things that you have been passionate about; then read them out loud. Writing and reading out loud will utilize sight, touch, and

hearing to help imbed these into your mind. (If passion is too strong a word, write down things you've liked doing or seeing.) Post both your big dream for this month and your interests or passions in a good place for you to be reminded on occasion during the day. This is your list.

Challenge for Today:

Really, try being silly and giggling sometime soon!

Day 3

Day 3 Quote:

Think about your goals and review them daily. Every morning when you begin, take action on the most important task you can accomplish to achieve your most important goal at the moment.
—Brian Tracy

Insight:

By taking a few minutes to settle ourselves and allow space to just be quiet at the beginning of our day (perhaps even hear from God), we can then think. We gain a much better perspective on what is truly important that day and how to set up the day to be more successful.

When taking action on that most important task first, you feel so much better that you've either progressed with it or accomplished it, and everything else seems to flow. As Brian Tracy advocates in his book *Eat That Frog*, doing the toughest item on your list first helps you overcome procrastination. Love yourself enough to give yourself that time early in the day, and take action on it.

Actions to Take for Day 3:

1. Say out loud while looking in the mirror, "I love you. God loves you."
2. Read your dream out loud.
3. If you want to, add three more things to your list from yesterday of your passions or likes, and then read it out loud. When you remind yourself of those things that you like, enjoy, or are passionate about, you can begin to include them in your day on a more regular basis.
4. Remember your goal that you originally set? Find a good place to post that goal list (if you haven't already) where you will see it frequently during the day—your calendar, mirror, or fridge. You want that friendly reminder. You are practicing awareness. The more you can be aware of your thoughts, your goals, and the things you love, the more often they will happen. Quite simply, you will remember to watch for them!

Challenge for Today:

Find a motivational book to begin reading. A short one that I love is *Rhinoceros Success* by Scott Alexander.

Day 4

Day 4 Quote:

He who gets wisdom loves his own soul; he who keeps understanding will find good.
—Proverbs 19:8, NKJV

Insight:

When we are seeking wisdom, the Bible says that we love ourselves. Wisdom is out there for us to seek after, find, and keep. I heard a great definition for wisdom: it's knowledge applied. It's information that we learn that we can then use. It's practical. It's useful. It can stay in our memory. It's the stuff we did that actually worked! It's a phenomenal tool at our disposal when we remember to be quiet and seek it. It adds so much to the quality of our lives.

Have you picked up some wisdom today, discovered how to use a new mental tool? Think of it as a special insight that makes things simpler to do or easier to bear. Another way to understand it would be calling it a "positive perspective." Sometimes a very simple tweak on an idea changes your perspective on the way you deal with it.

A movie called *The Gods Must Be Crazy* came out years ago about a Coke bottle that ended up in a primitive tribal setting. The tribe members didn't know the actual function, so it was used for all kinds of things and highly valued. We too can look at everyday items and ideas and try using them in new ways. Add to your wisdom.

Actions to Take for Day 4:

1. Say out loud to yourself, "I love you," and "God loves you."
2. Remind yourself of your goal from day 1. Keep reading it out loud.
3. Also, if you happen to think of a passion or something you like, add it to your list. It doesn't have to end—ever!

Challenge for Today:

As you go through your day, look for everyday items that you could re-purpose. Think of other possible uses. Try to find three items with a new idea, or one item with three ideas. Write them down.

NOTES

Day 5

Day 5 Quotes:

We lift ourselves by our thought. We climb upon our vision of ourselves. If you want to enlarge your life, you must first enlarge your thought of it and of yourself. Hold the ideal of yourself as you long to be, always everywhere.
                    —Orison Swett Marden

For as he thinketh in his heart, so is he.
                    —Proverbs 23:7

Insight:

We lift ourselves by our thoughts. The opposite is also true. Keep tabs on those thoughts! Get rid of the negative ones. Don't allow them any time in your head. Change the thoughts to something positive as soon as you notice them (you'll get faster over time).

We can hold ourselves in a good light and picture a life that we want. God gave us a powerful mind that has the ability to hold a vision. The mind works in pictures. The longer we hold those thoughts or pictures, the closer we are to becoming what we hold on to. God also wants abundance and health for us. He wants us to get the negatives out of our heads and focus on the positives. Our thoughts are directly tied to the words we use. Brain scans actually show that positive words increase connectivity and hit our main pleasure center to create positive energy in our bodies, so we feel the words too. What comes out of our mouths is very important for both ourselves (we hear it too) and others.

Actions to Take for Day 5:

1. Say out loud while looking in the mirror, "I love you. God loves you."
2. Read your dream out loud too.
3. Give out some positivity. Say something nice (and mean it because people can tell) to someone today. Try saying something nice to yourself too.

Challenge for Today:

Give yourself a quota of how many people you are going to say something nice to today.

Day 6

Day 6 Quote:

Just as your car runs more smoothly and requires less energy to go faster and farther when the wheels are in perfect alignment, you perform better when your thoughts, feelings, emotions, goals, and values are in balance.

—Brian Tracy

Insight:

This principle applies to our bodies and minds. When our legs are weak, our balance is off, and we can fall and do ourselves physical harm. When we are faithful to strengthen ourselves on a daily basis, we are ready for anything! It's important to spend the time to align our thought muscles as well so that they are also strong and ready. That is really loving ourselves. Whatever your faith may be, reading about it will help your mind align to it to a greater degree, enabling you to keep your faith balance strengthened.

Actions to Take for Day 6:

1. Say, "I love you. God loves you."
2. Remind yourself of your goal from day 1. Keep reading it out loud.
3. Also, if you happen to think of something really fun you'd like to do, add it to your list. We hear great ideas all the time. Remember that it doesn't have to end—ever!
4. Another great exercise to do for further alignment and mental strength is to make a list of your positive attributes, abilities, and character strengths. Sometimes we have a challenge when coming up with nice things about ourselves. Ask trusted family and friends to help with this—something about you that they admire. Write them out by hand, and then read them out loud. List positive attributes and strengths that you would like to have as well.

Challenge for Today:

Look at your list of positive attributes, abilities, and character strengths and find which ones mean the most to you. Do something today to utilize it consciously.

_____
_____
_____
_____
_____
_____
_____
_____
_____
_____
_____
_____
_____
_____
_____
_____
_____
_____
_____
_____
_____
_____
_____
_____
_____
_____
_____
_____
_____

Day 7

Day 7 Quote:

You miss 100 percent of the shots you never take.
—Wayne Gretzky

First things first—yay! You've made it to the end of one week! Congratulations! Now for the insight.

Insight:

My daughter Lydia was about forty feet up in a pine tree. She didn't like heights, but she was doing it anyway. What shots do you want to take? What new things do you want to do or try? We all have those things hidden away in our hearts. Take a peek in there and see what they are. Instead of saying "I can't," say "Why not?" (If you watch the movie *We Bought a Zoo*, it'll add depth and fun to why not?). People have always regretted the things they did not try in life more than the things they did, even if they didn't succeed every time.

Actions to Take for Day 7:

1. Say, "I love you. God loves you."
2. Remind yourself of your goal from day 1. Keep reading it out loud.
3. Keep adding to your passion list as you think of things.
4. Rewrite your list of positive attributes, abilities, and character strengths by hand, then read it out loud.

Challenge for Today:

Take a Shot! This may very well be the key that changes everything for you.

Step 1: Think of three things that you have thought about trying in the past, and for one reason or another, they got shot down. Make your list. Don't yet look at the reasons why you've told yourself no.

Step 2: Which of those three things really resonates with you and you feel yourself getting excited about trying? It's okay if you also feel a little scared. Look at that one in more depth now. Ask yourself why you did not do it in the past. Examine what may be holding you back, and write down all the reasons.

Step 3: Ask yourself whether it is something ridiculous. Sometimes it is. Is it a somewhat valid reason? Figure out a work-around, even if it's only a small step.

Step 4: Write down three reasons why you can do it—why it's not ridiculous!

Step 5: Make a plan with three things that you can do to follow that pursuit and a reasonable time line to do them. Make sure one of those three is really easy and something you can do quickly today.

Step 6: Do it. Take the shot!

NOTES

Day 8

Day 8 Quote:

Taking time for yourself should never be seen as a burden. Not on you, and not on anyone else.
—Elizabeth Franklin

Insight:

Are you seeing this as a burden? You may want to discover why. Have fun with this and act like a four-year-old to answer the "Why is this a burden to me?" question five times. That usually gets to the heart of the matter or makes you exasperated with your four-year-old you! It is actually a process tool used in industry to get to the root of an issue. When you have the whys, you are better able to deal with them.

Now ask yourself why it might be a blessing to take time for yourself. Also write down why taking time for yourself is important—at least five really good reasons that make you smile. It's not enough just to tell yourself to do or not to do something. It needs to be meaningful for you and tied to your values in order to get done. We're still working on alignment. Get everything tracking on the same peaceful path. Make sure that your vision is in alignment with your values, those things that are important to you. The closer that alignment, the easier it will be to enlarge your life and become everything you dream of. That alignment boosts your motivation.

Actions to Take for Day 8:

1. Say, "I love you. God loves you."
2. Remind yourself of your goal from day 1. Keep reading it out loud.
3. Keep adding to your passion list as you think of things.
4. Make a list of your top values. A helpful way to do this is to find the list on my website and find your top ten to fifteen from the list. How will you know whether you are in alignment with what you really hold dear if you are not clear on exactly what those things are and their level of importance in your life? Be clear to be in alignment.

Challenge for Today:

What are your top three values? You may even want to write out why they are the top three. It is important that the reasons make you feel good.

Day 9

Day 9 Quote:

Keep your face to the sunshine and you will not see the shadows.
—Helen Keller

Insight:

Wow! The first time I read this, I saw the perspective that only Helen Keller could bring to this quote. The light and energy and warmth that come from the sun are so powerful and infusing.

Stop right now and close your eyes and turn your face to the sunshine (or a light, if it's nighttime). For comparison, turn away, and then turn back to the sun again and stay for a few moments to soak this in. Just notice how you feel.

It reminds me of a Scripture verse, 1 John 1:5: "This then is the message which we have heard of him, and declare unto you, that God is light, and in him is no darkness at all." If this verse is true, why would we ever want to turn away? Keep smiling to bring out your own sunshine, or Son-shine.

Actions to Take for Day 9:

1. Say, "I love you. God loves you."
2. Remind yourself of your goal from day 1. Keep reading it out loud.
3. Keep adding to your passion list as you think of things.
4. You have been rewriting your list of positive attributes, abilities, and character strengths by hand and then reading it out loud. Now we are changing it up just a little to add more of the five senses and fun, which will help it get ingrained deeper into your subconscious mind, where it becomes a part of you. You are training your brain to track the way you want it to—not the way the newspapers, TV, and other influences would have you do. Once a day, read your list out loud while doing some or all of the following:
   - Stand or sit with great posture.
   - Have great inspirational music playing.
   - Walk around or dance!
   - Light a scented candle.

Challenge for Today:
Now practice being that light. Radiate!

NOTES

Day 10

Day 10 Quote:

We have a duty to encourage one another. Many a time a word of praise or thanks or appreciation or cheer has kept a man on his feet. Blessed is the man who speaks such a word.
—William Barclay

Insight:

Remember to be your own best friend. Yes, your friend would encourage you, praise you, thank you, acknowledge and appreciate you. And you would do those same things for a friend anytime. You can do this for yourself as well.

In the picture, our daughter made the faces of different Shakespearean characters on fruits for a school project—brilliant fun! Acknowledge and value the character that you are. God does!

Actions to Take for Day 10:
1. Say, "I love you." And remember, it's because God loves you!
2. Remind yourself of your goal from day 1. Keep reading it out loud.
3. Keep adding to your passion list as you think of things.
4. We are continuing to do the same things. You have been rewriting your list of positive attributes, abilities, and character strengths by hand and then reading it out loud. Also remember to change it up just a little to add more of the five senses and therefore ingrain it deeper into your subconscious mind, where it becomes a part of you. A challenge is added for you as well (see below).

Challenge for Today:
Step 1: Write down two encouragements, two praises, two things you can thank yourself for, and two things that you appreciate in yourself, just since the time you began the "thirty days." Smile while you do it.

Step 2: Give encouragement, praise, or a compliment to someone else today. Try to do it face-to-face if you can. It's much more meaningful and influential.

Day 11

Day 11 Quote:

Real optimism is aware of problems, but recognizes solutions; knows about difficulties, but believes they can be overcome; sees the negatives, but accentuates the positives; is exposed to the worst, but expects the best; has reason to complain, but chooses to smile.
—William Arthur Ward

*Day 11 Photo:

Meet my friend Kay. She and I watched our nutrition together and worked out at 5:30 a.m. 5 days a week for several years. She started out at 238 pounds, taking 4 blood-pressure meds and at 190/105. She almost quit at the beginning, even knowing that she was in a life-or-death struggle. My son Jeremy, doing the hand slap at the right, is her personal trainer and convinced her to continue. She did. In 2 years, she has lost 85 pounds and is off 3 of those meds and maintains a very healthy blood pressure of 105/70. Kay began her journey when she was in her 60s. She ran the 5K portion of a local triathlon event this fall (2012). She is an inspiration to me, and I wanted her in this book to be an example for you of real optimism. Kay rocks!

Insight:

Real optimism is not Pollyanna-ish, with our heads in the clouds. Real optimists are realists who have a clear focus of what they want in their lives and control their thoughts to accomplish it. Optimists live five to seven years longer, and they have more fun while living too.

Learning to control our thoughts better and better each day is also loving and respecting ourselves. It becomes a habit and easier with continued practice (you may note, I'm telling myself too).

Actions to Take for Day 11:

1. Say, "I love you. God loves you."
2. Remind yourself of your goal from day 1. Keep reading it out loud.
3. Keep adding to your passion list as you think of things.
4. We are continuing to do the same things. You have been rewriting your list of positive attributes, abilities, and character strengths by hand and then reading it out loud. Also remember to change it up just a little to add more of the five senses and

therefore ingrain it deeper into your subconscious mind, where it becomes a part of you. Exercise teaches your brain that behavior makes a difference. Repetition is important too. A new challenge is added for you as well (see below).

Challenge for Today:

Too often we have a lot of negative self-talk in our heads and not nearly enough positive self-talk. To help you with that, at the end of the day, write down at least one thing you did that you feel good about. You can write as many as you like and three to five is best. This is a practice that, when done faithfully, changes lives.

NOTES

This is one of my reasons for making healthy decisions and thinking things through. I want to be around for my grandchildren for a long time.

Day 12

Day 12 Quote:

Our own well-being is always the result of healthy decisions for ourselves coupled with disengagement from the choices of others.
—Karen Casey

Insight:

Are you beginning to make more and more healthy decisions? They are healthy for you when they are in alignment with your values. You feel complete and whole when in alignment.

It's challenging because we don't live in a vacuum. We do encounter other influences in our daily lives. Others' choices may not be healthy for us, and the people may have a toxic attitude to go along with it. It is sometimes challenging to do the right thing when faced with the choice to do so.

When confronted with unhealthy behavior that we don't want, it is important to think of the positive choice that we would like to make and to remember all the reasons that we do those things. We look at the person making the negative choice and what it's doing in their life. That usually makes it very easy to disengage ourselves from that negative behavior and choice.

When it comes right down to it, do we really care what others think, or do we care more about what positive things we want for our lives? Yay for loving yourself enough to take a stand!

Actions to Take for Day 12:

1. Say to yourself, "I love you. God loves you." It really is important to remember!
2. Remind yourself of your dream from day 1. Keep reading it out loud. I hope you are remembering to add it to your daily to-do list and to take action.
3. Keep adding to your passion list as you think of things. Do some!
4. We are continuing to do the same things, small but powerful building blocks. You have been rewriting your list of positive attributes, abilities, and character strengths by hand and then reading it out loud.

Challenge for Today:

Add more of the five senses activities like we listed on day 9. What "five senses activities" did you choose? Are you doing anything new?

NOTES

Day 13

Day 13 Quote:

It takes a lot of work from the face to let out a smile, but just think what good smiling can bring to the most important muscle of the body—the heart.

—Author unknown

Insight:

I read that this is absolutely true. Smiling does good things for your heart! It sometimes does take some work to let out a smile, like when we're passing someone on the street and not knowing if they'll smile back or not. When smiling, good endorphins are produced, and the pleasure center of the brain responds (even when we don't really mean it!) to make us feel good. God really knew what He was doing when He set up our wiring!

Actions to Take for Day 13:

1. Yes, again, every day! It really does make a difference when you do this faithfully. Say, "I love you. God loves you."
2. Remind yourself of your goal from day 1. Keep reading it out loud.
3. Keep adding to your passion list as you think of things.
4. Yup, these are the same things again! Remember that I said repetition is one of the ways we train our brains? You have been rewriting your list of positive attributes, abilities, and character strengths by hand and then reading it out loud. Also remember to change it up just a little to add more of the five senses and therefore ingrain it deeper into your subconscious mind, where it becomes a part of you.

Are you smiling as you go about your day? If you find that you aren't, try to put that smile back on. Find someone who really needs it, and give it to them. It's free!

Challenge for Today:
See how many people will smile when you give them a smile today. Make it a game and keep track.

My family likes to laugh and smile often. Smiles are infectious, so I'm hoping you have a smile on now too, even if it's just on the inside. It still counts!

NOTES

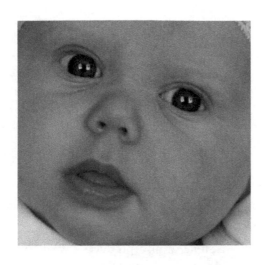

Day 14

Day 14 Quote:

A smile costs nothing but gives much. It enriches those who receive without making poorer those who give. It takes but a moment, but the memory of it sometimes lasts forever. None is so rich or mighty that he cannot get along without it, and none is so poor that he cannot be made rich by it. Yet a smile cannot be bought, begged, borrowed, or stolen, for it is something that is of no value to anyone until it is given away. Some people are too tired to give you a smile.

Give them one of yours, as none needs a smile so much as he who has no more to give.
—Author unknown

You made it to two weeks! Yay! Keep it up!

Insight:

It's hard to smile too much, so I thought I'd throw it in two days in a row! Is your face sore yet from smiling so much? Did you know that it takes more muscles to frown than to smile?

When we give a smile, it also produces that awesome response in the pleasure center of our brain. Do you need another reason? That's one you may not have thought of, but again, we're hardwired this way. God wants us to give, so He set us up so that we'd also have a benefit—immediately!

Pay it forward. Keep smiling, even when you don't feel like it.

Actions to Take for Day 14:

1. Step out in action and go beyond just smiling. Figure out a way to unexpectedly delight someone today. God will show you a way. It'll pay off in abundance for you and the recipient. You will be smiling.

2. And remember to give away lots of smiles again today!

Challenge for Today:

Write down what you did today to unexpectedly delight someone. It will bring you a smile every time you read it.

NOTES

Day 15

Day 15 Quote:

Life does not consist mainly, or even largely, of facts and happenings. It consists mainly of the storm of thought that is forever flowing through one's head.

—Mark Twain

Insight:

What storms have you had in your head lately? Notice I'm not asking you IF you've had any storms lately. We all have storms. It is human nature.

What is important is what we do with those storms. Do we let them build and build until we have a hurricane? Do we let them blow out over the ocean of calm that we bring to ourselves by again finding our quiet place and remembering to take care of ourselves and to love ourselves? Take the time to quiet your storms. That still, small voice will be there when the storm is quiet.

Actions to Take for Day 15:

Are you beginning to enjoy this time that you are giving yourself? It's only a few minutes, but it reaps so much more in your quality of life. Yes, this is redundant, and that's exactly the point. I gave you a break yesterday!

1. Say, "I love you. God loves you."
2. Remember your passion list.
3. Read your list of attributes out loud twice every day, once when you get up and again right before you go to bed. Sit or stand with great posture and a big smile on your face. Try to remember the environment from the prior week. Can you smell the candle, hear the music, feel the air breeze by as you walk, etc.? Acknowledge your senses. God gave you those too! It really is meant to be enjoyable.

Challenge for Today:

Find a quiet place and just breathe. Calm yourself and then capture your thoughts. Are you noticing any shifts in your thinking? What are you noticing?

Day 16

Be pitiful [compassionate, kind], for every man is fighting a hard battle.

—John Watson

Insight:

Sometimes there are situations in which we are offended in some way. Usually it is unintentional, and this quote helps us to deal with those situations. It really doesn't matter what the other person said or did. It matters what you do with it.

We are often very good at hiding our battles, pain, and scars from each other. The offender very well could be doing that, and the scars may be invisible.

There are many people in pain in our world—mentally, physically, and spiritually. Holidays can be an especially challenging time. We need to remember to be kind and to not be too easily offended. Don't take it personally, and give it to God.

We can be like the faithful dog, always there to greet us and make us feel good by accepting us just the way we are. Accept others as they are. Don't be offended. The dog is man's best friend. Shouldn't we be friends to each other on this level?

Actions to Take for Day 16:

You've made it this far! You. Nobody can do it for you. They can encourage you or ask you if you've done it, but only you can value yourself enough to do what it takes. Ultimately, it's not about reading self-help books or going to seminars. It's about doing what it takes. That means sometimes doing the uncomfortable. It becomes more comfortable with time. You have the heart to do it. Now keep taking the steps. It's really about the quality you add to this time—not just getting through it.

1. Say, "I love you. God loves you."
2. Read your goal or dream.
3. Keep adding to your passion list. Do some of them.
4. Remember to radiate!

Challenge for Today:

Take a big step. Ask yourself what is holding you back. Capture your thoughts in the notes section.

Day 17

Day 17 Quote:

Motherhood is near to divinity. It's the highest, holiest service to be assumed by mankind.
>—Howard W. Hunter

Insight:

I have a wonderful mom in my life. She loves gardening. We still go to a garden show together each year, and we also let each other know when our daffodils are up. I have to tour her yard at different times of the growing season, and she does the same with mine. Our relationship is different from when I was growing up. Then it was . . .

"Go get some fresh air. It's good for you."

"Do you need to pee?"

"Want me to kiss it and make it better?"

"Not before dinner—you'll spoil your appetite."

"Don't sit so close to the TV; it's bad for your eyes."

"Good night, sleep tight, sweet dreams."

When we were young, we were looked after. As we get older, sometimes we forget to look after ourselves. Self-care is so important for our lives. If we don't do it as adults, it won't get done.

Have fun and a sense of humor with life. When looking after yourself, remember to lighten up. Go get some fresh air, close your mouth, and pee when you need to (smile)! Kiss it yourself if you have to, and heavens, don't snack before dinner or sit too close to the TV!

Be your own caregiver. Enjoy your life—even the little moments—and remember to have a good night, sleep tight, and have sweet dreams.

Actions to Take for Day 17:

1. Say, "I love you. God loves you."

2. What is something that you've neglected to do for yourself lately? Stop what you're doing right now. Put it on the schedule, make the phone call or whatever it takes, and get it done. There now, don't you feel better?

3. And don't forget your list! Take good care of yourself. Love yourself. I'm not writing it out this time. I'm hoping that you're starting to make it a habit. Do you remember it? Do you remember why you're doing it? It's because God loves you.

Challenge for Today:

If you still have your mother, acknowledge her in some way today. If not, acknowledge someone who is a mother.

> *Be still, and know that I am God: I will be*
> *exalted among the heathen, I will be exalted in*
> *the earth!*
>
> —Psalm 46:10, NKJV

NOTES

Day 18

Day 18 Quote:

I am only one; but still I am one. I cannot do everything, but still I can do something. I will not refuse to do the something I can do.
—Helen Keller

Insight:

No, I didn't cut the tree down single-handedly! Just being silly. Think about someone that you love tremendously, whether it is a spouse, a child, or a friend. Take time to think about how wonderful that person is and how you feel about them. (Just follow my train of thought for a moment—we'll get to the point.) Note how it feels inside you—that warmth and tenderness. Take a moment to think about the last time or a special time when you did something for that person and how truly great that was. Think about how it made you feel.

Now think about being your own friend and appreciating yourself the same way that you appreciate the person you were just thinking about. Feel those same feelings of warmth and tenderness toward yourself. You are worth it, you know. Allow yourself to receive that love. Remember to do that for yourself when you are saying "I love you. God loves you" out loud. Here's the point. Do the something that you can do, no matter if you are old or young. You can begin by loving and respecting yourself. It always comes back to the simple things, even when we try to make them difficult.

Actions to Take for Day 18:

1. Say, "I love you. God loves you."
2. Continue doing all the things on the list. What steps are you taking toward your monthly goal today? Download a bookmark from my website that will help: http://www. YourGodGivenDignity.com
3. Also, take out the list of things you are passionate about or like. For each item, write down just one thing you could do that would help you incorporate it into your life immediately. Make it a simple, easy baby step. Take just one of those actions and do it today. You could even do it tomorrow too! Do the something that you can do!

Challenge for Today:

Were you able to love yourself the way you love others? Ask yourself why or why not and write that down. Also write down how you can be better at both loving yourself and others.

Day 19

Day 19 Quote:

Beloved, I wish above all things that thou mayest prosper and be in health, even as thy soul prospereth.

—3 John 1:2

Insight:

The thing I especially like about this scripture is that it calls us His beloved. Wow! Then it says that it is His wish—above all things, above everything else He has said that He wants for us—for us to prosper and be in health. That is gigantic! Awesome!

This is a love note from God. Prospering has a lot to do with thankfulness. It is an attitude of overall well-being. Being in health is not a halfway thing either; it's not being "un-sick." Health is that vibrancy, that glow, that strength that comes from giving our bodies the right things at the right time—food and exercise and love. If that is what God wants, then that is what we need to focus on for ourselves.

God shows us that He loves us in His words to us. What are our words and actions that show our love? What are our words to ourselves? Do our words mirror His? Are we still reminding ourselves that we are who God says we are? We are His lights in this world. Are we reminding others that they also are bright lights?

Remember to radiate.

Actions to Take for Day 19:

1. Say, "I love you. God loves you."
2. Is there anything that you do for your health daily? Do whatever the heck you want! The only stipulation is—besides being moral and ethical and loving to yourself—it has to be fun enough to make you laugh! It would be nice to brighten up someone else's day too. Reflect. How did you radiate health and prosperity of attitude today?

Challenge for Today:

What is one new thing that you can do today to increase your overall prosperity that includes health and well-being? Even if it's a baby step, take it. Step out.

NOTES

Day 20

Day 20 Quote:

Most folks are about as happy as they make up their minds to be.
—Abraham Lincoln

Insight:

When someone says, "I woke up on the wrong side of the bed today," it's just an excuse for what they chose that didn't go well. Maybe they just don't want to change their mind. Have you ever heard anyone say that they woke up on the *right* side of bed?

No matter which side of the bed we get out of, every day is a choice, and every moment is a choice. The choice is ours. There is a lot of freedom in that. There is also a lot of responsibility. It's who we chose to be.

What we generate also rubs off onto others. Consider your impact. Do you want to be the black cloud, or do you want to bring the light? Be aware. If you know someone who has an attitude you don't want to rub off on you, spend less time interacting with them, or show them that they also have a choice to "get up on the right side."

As Abe says, it's what you make up your mind to be.

Actions to Take for Day 20:
1. Read your list and then say, "I love you. God loves you."
2. Read your goal.
3. Keep adding to your passion list. Do some of them.
4. Remember to radiate!

Challenge for Today:
It is said that you become like the five people you spend most of your time with. Think about that. Who are your five? How do they make you feel? Do you need to think about upgrading or just spending time in a different place? Write down five people you know that you respect. See if it's possible to spend time with them on occasion.

NOTES

_____
_____
_____
_____
_____
_____
_____
_____
_____
_____
_____
_____
_____
_____
_____
_____
_____
_____
_____
_____
_____
_____
_____
_____
_____
_____
_____

Day 21

Day 21 Quote:

For a long time it had seemed to me that life was about to begin—real life. But there was always some obstacle in the way, something to be gotten through first, some unfinished business, time still to be served, a debt to be paid. Then life would begin. At last it dawned on me that these obstacles were my life.

—Alfred D. Souza

Insight:

Three weeks in and I am thankful for you! I hope you are remembering to be thankful to God for yourself. Sometimes the obstacles remind us to be thankful. My husband found an obstacle with the ATV and I am thankful to have him!

The number 21, as in day 21, made me think about what and how we think when we are young—that it's all about us. When we're sixteen, we want to be a high school graduate. When we're a grad, we want to be twenty-one, legal, and an adult. Next we want to be on our own, married, and to have children, etc. And at some point, we want to turn the clock back and be a kid again!

Every time we turn around there's a new experience and something to learn to equip us for the road ahead, and we're always working to get somewhere, to the next thing. We feel invincible and have boundless energy at twenty-one, but there are so many unknowns and so many obstacles that it often seems overwhelming and very stressful as well. Finding ourselves and finding what we're going to be are what it is about. There is always one more thing to do, and then someday it'll be just the way we want it.

Then this pattern becomes a lifestyle. But at some point we have to stop and say, "Hey, wait! This is life! Enjoy this moment!" Don't you wish that we could convey this wisdom to the young—or to ourselves when we get too busy, challenged, or frustrated?

It's a wonderful realization when it hits, that it's the journey and the joy we take in that journey that makes up life. The details, the moments, the now—it's nice to be reminded to stop and smell the roses. It's nice to take a deep breath and enjoy the moment. Enjoy being you today, even if you're not twenty-one. Enjoy that you've made it through, over, or in spite of the obstacles, and that maybe you've learned something in the process.

Actions to Take for Day 21:

1.   Say, "I love you. God loves you."
2.   Read your goal.
3.   Keep adding to your passion list. Do some of them.
4.   Remember to radiate!

Challenge for Today:

Think of some way to remind yourself to stop and enjoy the moment. You could think of a phrase that reminds you that you can repeat to yourself throughout the day. It could be a personal motto. Write down a phrase that you think might work for you and post it where you will see it frequently. If you add your phrase to a meaningful picture, it will work even better.

Day 22

Day 22 Quote:

That Christ may dwell in your hearts by faith; that ye, being rooted and grounded in love.

—Ephesians 3:17

Insight:

Have you ever really stopped to consider what this verse really means for you in terms of love? It says that Christ—the man who did miracles, wonders, and signs because of His obedience to His Father, God—may dwell in our hearts. The word dwell makes me think of a home where you have comfort and safety. Our hearts are His home.

Then those two words, "by faith," we can understand to mean "by believing." We believe that Jesus Christ came and died for us and that God raised Him. That enables us to have Christ in us. Where did you think the word "Christian" came from?

When we realize just how much we are loved, having Christ dwelling in our hearts is very warming and comforting—the bigness of it, the privilege of it—and all we did was believe, and accept it. This is the comfort that was promised. Then it says that you are rooted and grounded in love. That's your foundation and where you draw your nourishment and strength. If you think of a plant being rooted and grounded, you can think of how strong it is. It's nice to think of yourself having that same strong foundation of love and comfort from God that you can draw from as you go about your day. Would God give His children any less than He gives a plant? What strength! In writing this, I realized that I need to be reminded of this too!

Actions to Take for Day 22:

1. Say, "I love you. God loves you."
2. Read your goal.
3. Keep adding to your passion list. Do some of them.
4. Remember to radiate!

Challenge for Today:

Instead of thinking on mistakes, errors, faux pas, etc., try to remember all the good of the day. Acknowledge yourself for what you did right. Write down at least five of them. Give credit where credit is due. Respect and love yourself for your strengths and victories.

Day 23

Day 23 Quote:

Appreciative words are the most powerful force for good on earth.
—George W. Crane

Insight:

These aren't just two sweet-looking older people. They are my stepdad and my mom. He is continually saying nice things about my mom to anyone who will listen. It's even nice for me to hear! I like knowing that my mom is appreciated by her other half. She deserves that. In honoring them here, I want to say that my stepdad is an awesome bass guitarist, and my mom is a super believer and giver.

What appreciative words have you given today? Did you remember to give some to yourself? Before you go any further in your day, think of two things that you appreciate about yourself and hold that in your thoughts for a while.

A special person in my life shared with me that when you think something nice about someone, those nice thoughts aren't just yours. They are meant to be spoken and shared with that person. That has helped me to be bolder in speaking up to others.

Actions to Take for Day 23:

1. Say, "I love you. God loves you."
2. Read your goal.
3. Keep adding to your passion list. Do some of them.
4. Remember to radiate!
5. List five personal acknowledgments as explained in the day 22 challenge.

Challenge for Today:

Find one or two people in the course of your day that you can give sincere, appreciative words to. You'll make their day and your own. Making something a habit for a lifetime requires many little things each day. Let someone know what you are working on, and ask that person to hold you accountable by asking you, with concern and without judgment, how it's going on a regular basis (like once a week). You'll want to give them a truthful, positive report. Integrity with yourself is key.

NOTES

_____

_____

_____

_____

_____

_____

_____

_____

_____

_____

_____

_____

_____

_____

_____

_____

_____

_____

_____

_____

_____

_____

_____

_____

_____

_____

_____

_____

Day 24

Day 24 Quotes:

There came a time when the risk to remain tight in the bud was more painful than the risk it took to blossom.
—Anais Nin

Life is a process of becoming, a combination of states we have to go through. Where people fail is that they wish to elect a state and remain in it. This is a kind of death.
—Anais Nin

Insight:

Doubt, worry, and fear are usually what keep us from taking chances and trying new things. Doing something new is a risk, but without taking that risk, we stagnate.

Daffodils are my younger daughter's favorite flower. They bloom around her birthday every year. This picture was taken when we took her for a drive on her birthday instead of just doing the traditional birthday party. We took a risk. We took her to Highland Park in Rochester, New York, which was just full of daffodils. She loved it!

What new thing are you doing for yourself today? Are you taking a risk, trying something new, and really living your life? If you are not ready to do this, ask yourself what your doubts are or what you are worried about. Tackle it and free yourself to bloom.

Actions to Take for Day 24:

1. Say, "I love you. God loves you."
2. Read your goal.
3. Keep adding to your passion list. Do some of them.
4. Remember to radiate!
5. List five more personal acknowledgments as explained in the day 22 challenge.

Challenge for Today:

Examine your goal again from day 1. What is something new you have wanted to do with this? Write down what you think has been holding you back. What are your doubts? Some of them may be quite valid. Listen to them and think of ways to satisfy those doubts while still pursuing your new project. Doubts can be helpful if we use them, rather than allow them to stop us.

Day 25

Day 25 Quote:

All change is not growth, as all movement is not forward.
—Ellen Glasgow

Insight:

When ice forms thickly on a twig and everything is frozen, we see change without growth—other than more and more ice! We all seem to want change, until it comes and we notice it's not the change we ordered. We know for sure that change for the sake of change is not what we want.

I'm sure you've heard the saying that we take one step forward, two steps back, and it sometimes seems like that when we are trying to change. Sometimes this is true, but as we persevere, it becomes two steps forward, one step back, and we begin building momentum. Perseverance builds momentum even when we aren't seeing any apparent movement forward. It will come. Rest in that knowledge. Momentum can be a powerful source of motivation.

Actions to Take for Day 25:

1. Say, "I love you. God loves you."
2. Read your goal.
3. Keep adding to your passion list. Do some of them.
4. Remember to radiate!
5. List five more personal acknowledgments.

Challenge for Today:

What are you going to take a step forward on today to show that you are loving yourself and bringing good change? If you are this far, you have already been taking steps forward! You are being faithful to persevere. I want to encourage you to continue to persevere, even when you don't see something happening. It often happens behind the scenes. Be patient. Take a deep breath and know that it's okay. Keep taking the steps. The process is the most important part.

*

~~~~~

Day 26

~~~~~

Day 26 Quotes:

Nothing tastes as good as thin feels.
　　　　　　　—Author unknown

Don't trade what you want most for what you want now.
　　　　　　　—Author unknown

You can never be too rich or too thin.
　　　　　　　—Duchess of Windsor

Insight:

These are some quotes that helped me get through my weight-loss journey. Everyone has a journey that they are on in life, and it is important to find inspiration wherever you can. If you are also on a weight-loss journey and these quotes resonate with you and can help you too, then keep them where you can see them often to remind yourself of what you truly want.

I did get to my goal weight, but it didn't happen overnight. I had to fight with my mind! Thin really does feel good, and it's really worth making the right choices to get there. Delaying gratification is a huge key in any success journey. Don't cash in too quickly; remind yourself why you are doing this, and often, especially when you are angry or emotional.

I added the third quote just for fun and partly because some people would try to sabotage my dream by saying that I was thin enough or that I wasn't fat. If I wasn't where I wanted to be, then I couldn't be dissuaded from my goal, even if it didn't suit them. We have to remember to have fun along the way, and this was just a fun way to overcome that objection.

Actions to Take for Day 26:

1. Say, "I love you. God loves you."
2. Read your goal.
3. Keep adding to your passion list. Do some of them.
4. Remember to radiate!
5. List five more personal acknowledgments.

Challenge for Today:

Delay gratification of some small thing today, and once you do have it or do it, notice how much more you appreciate it. Savor that.

*Day 26 Photos:

When I saw the first picture, something clicked in my head. I was not happy inside, and my body was not happy or healthy. I said to myself, I'm going to use that disgusting picture to change my habits and remind myself of where I came from. I'm going to get healthy, happy, and slim! I lost thirty-five pounds, going from 32 percent to 23 percent body fat. Yay!

Day 27

Day 27 Quote:

Now unto him that is able to do exceeding abundantly above all that we ask or think, according to the power that worketh in us.
—Ephesians 3:20

Insight:

I love this verse. It starts out very simply saying that God is able, and that is a nice reminder in itself, especially when we are feeling vulnerable.

Then it goes on to say what He is able to do: exceeding abundantly above all that we ask or think!

Say that fast, then say it slowly—out loud. Any one of those words taken by itself would be amazing: Exceeding—that's big! Above—that's big too! Abundantly—I'll take it! How about all—a little word that packs a big punch! Put together, these words are just mind-boggling. It's even more mind-boggling if you look at the Greek meaning of exceeding (*huper*), which means super. Way beyond need, it's more than we can even think or dream about. Then we have the Greek meaning of abundantly (*perissos*), which means superabundant in quantity and superior in quality. It adds another dimension.

Exceeding . . . abundantly . . . above . . . all . . . we . . . ask . . . or think . . . (pause and breathe).

It's not limited to only what we're asking; it also applies to what we're thinking. Wow! I need to pause and breathe again!

Then He tells us how He is able to do that: according to the power that works in us. You might be tempted to think that this in some way limits the above concept. It does not. God is not only able but also willing. How willing? He sent His only begotten Son to die for you and me to be joint-heirs with Christ. All of the power (*dunamis*—the English word dynamite comes from that root word—that's power!) that Jesus exhibited as he walked on the earth is also ours. We can give, love, and heal in a very big way. I hope you are as excited reading this as I was in writing it. Pause and breathe. Christ in us is the glory of the mystery that once was hidden but now is revealed. He was the firstborn of many. It is our inheritance, our privilege, and, above all, our responsibility.

Actions to Take for Day 27:

1. Say, "I love you. God loves you."
2. Read your goal.
3. Keep adding to your passion list. Do some of them.

4. Remember to radiate!
5. List five more personal acknowledgments.

Challenge for Today:

Take time to remember all the wonderful events in your life so far. Write down one or two of them that meant the most to you and why. The thankfulness you generate by doing this is the building block for God's abundance in your life.

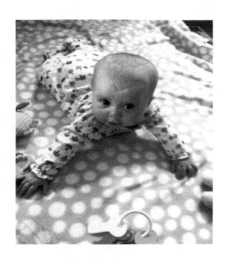

Day 28

Day 28 Quote:

It is the nature of man to rise to greatness if greatness is expected of him.

—John Steinbeck

Insight:

God is great. God has given us His greatness through His Son, Jesus Christ. Just as we expect greatness of our children and grandchildren, God expects greatness of us. He is loving and patient in bringing that greatness to its full fruition. There is no rush. We are a work in progress, and each one of us has something uniquely wonderful to give to the world.

Be patient with yourself. Love yourself. How would you work with a child or another person? Be kind and gentle to yourself too. Simply keep at it day after day without judgment. You are a labor of love, and the greatness of what God has for you will come. You are at the right place and the right time. You're reading this, aren't you? God believes in you! You are worthy. You are loved.

Actions to Take for Day 28:

1. Say, "I love you. God loves you." He gave His only begotten Son.
2. Read your goal.
3. Keep adding to your passion list. Do some of them.
4. Remember to radiate!
5. List five more personal acknowledgments.

Challenge for Today:

Congratulations for completing twenty-eight days—four weeks! Do something to celebrate: a high five? A happy dance? Remember that you are loved.

Day 29

Day 29 Quote:

It's not about what happens. It's about perspective. I may not be able to change what takes place, but I can always choose to change my thinking.

—Michelle Sedas

Insight:

It's true. Whatever happens, happens. If it's less than optimal, that doesn't mean it's the end of the world or that we need to have a pity party or even a bad day. It all depends on what's happening in our upper story—our mind. If we allow our emotions to run wild, it may be all of those things. Instead, we can make our minds track with our goals and dreams, and we'll acknowledge that it's just a temporary setback.

The world tests us. God comes through (in Him there is no darkness). We learn to listen to God's voice. God is that solid rock that we can depend on, no matter what. We can continue to expect the best and change our thinking to reflect that. We become stronger with each victory. We can continue to remember that we are loved and will therefore act in a way that shows that we love ourselves as well. You and I make that choice in each situation.

If you have made it this far, you are doing well! If you are having challenges, I help people overcome them. Coaches are especially equipped to help people with personal-change efforts. Too often people give up. Don't give up.

You can achieve that goal with learnable skills, proven steps, and a newfound confidence born of encouragement and finding your value. Sound exciting? It is. You can believe in yourself to take new actions and get the change that you want.

Actions to Take for Day 29:

1. Say, "I love you. God loves you."
2. Read your goal.
3. Keep adding to your passion list. Do some of them.
4. Remember to radiate!
5. List five more personal acknowledgments.

Challenge for Today:

Do you have a short, empowering phrase that you can tell yourself to enable you no matter what you're feeling? Make up one that works for you. It could be a verse or just a few words of encouragement, like "You rock!" Mine is simply, "I can do this!" Find yours. Keep repeating it to yourself. It sure is better than beating up on yourself!

Day 30

Day 30 Quotes:

Some men see things as they are and say, "Why?" I dream of things that never were and say, "Why not?"
　　　　—George Bernard Shaw

But Jesus beheld them, and said unto them, With men this is impossible; but with God all things are possible.
　　　　—Matthew 19:26

Insight:

Was anything significant built overnight? Very few things that have stood the test of time were built quickly. Those projects that took time have proven to be worthwhile investments, as is their maintenance. Those quaint boathouses in the city of Canandaigua, New York, were built in the 1850s and have required maintenance over the years to still look as good as they do today. We require maintenance too! God created us body, soul, and spirit. That was a lot of work. We each took about nine months to get here. He left it to us to take care of the maintenance. Proper rest, healthy food, and what we feed on mentally and spiritually are our responsibility.

The scientific study of epigenetics has proven that it is nurture and not nature that has the most influence on our overall well-being. Following a plan to the best of our ability is the way to succeed. Leave judgment and feeling bad out of the equation; they hold us back. Be realistic. Figure out what can be done better, and then incorporate that into the plan.

We are to continue working hard, bettering ourselves. We are always a work in progress, so leave out the judgment. And what do we do when we get discouraged? We seek answers, help, and learning to overcome the obstacles we are faced with. We don't have to take it all on our shoulders either. There are others in our world who have the ability and willingness to help.

It is not promised to be easy. It is promised to be possible. Seek the possibilities. Do the maintenance. If God puts it on your heart and initiates those stirrings within you for something else, listen. Then act.

Actions to Take for Day 30:

1. Say, "I love you. God loves you."
2. Read your goal.
3. Keep adding to your passion list. Do some of them.

4. Remember to radiate!
5. List five more personal acknowledgments.

Challenge for Today:

Reflect on how far you've come in thirty days. Did you achieve all that you set out to achieve? What else is left? What is the next dream or the next phase of this dream? Write these things down. You can do the thirty days again, and again, and again. Continue to acknowledge your success and celebrate! What did you do to celebrate finishing?

Next Steps

I am confident that you have made progress if you are at this point, unless you just skipped over everything and only read the beginning and end of the book. Whatever works for you—really! If you took this day-by-day, following the guide and challenging yourself to do new things along the way, then this method has worked for you. It can be continued in a variety of ways:

1. If it didn't work for you by just reading it day-by-day, my suggestion to you is to break it down into bite-sized pieces: going through a month doing only the mirror exercise, going through a second month adding the five acknowledgments, then a third month with a specific goal and your passions list, and a fourth month practicing giving love out and radiating.

2. Or you can just start over at day 1 and go through it again, making sure that you have no judgment about how you perceive your prior performance. It's all growth. Each time you begin the process, you'll begin at a different place of growth and understanding.

3. You can also continue doing just the action practices to reinforce the new thoughts and renew your mind to think the way you want to think and to incorporate this new way of thinking into your life.

4. Another option involves having even more variety, more support, and more interaction by talking with me personally. If you have found it difficult to stay on task, this option works far better. You can sign up for support via the website to receive reminders—and encouragement! If you have stayed on task and you want more depth, more accountability, and someone who'll be listening and acknowledging you, then talking with me personally would fit the bill also.

Every athlete who truly excels has an excellent coach. Sometimes we have to seek out those who will be our mentors and coaches in order to reach the heights that we want in life. Seek out those whom you trust to have your best interests at heart and you know believe in you. Most of us need the strength that comes from that acknowledgment.

If you think of other ways that this might work for people, send me an e-mail. I'd love to pass it on. I hope you pass on this information as well. You can access supplemental materials that go along with this book on my special blog page: www.YourGodGivenDignity.com.

Evaluate what has worked for you going through this process. Also capture what hasn't worked, and write down what you'll want to do to change as you go forward.

In Thankfulness

I am truly thankful to so many people who helped see this through to completion. First, I am thankful to God for the inspiration.

I am also thankful to my husband, Ed, for his continued love, his ideas, his energy, his IT help, financial support, and for bringing me tea when I was working late.

I am thankful to my children for their support and insights that went into this book. I am thankful for my children in-love (most call them in-laws), Nathan and Sarah, for being just the right partners for my children. You are a blessing to my life as well.

I am thankful that I can add pictures of my grandchildren. I am thankful to everyone who read my manuscript, and who gave ideas, insights, support, encouragement, and their blessings to this book. My heart is overflowing, and I'm hoping it can flow into yours as you read and enjoy what is here for you.

In Closing

Over time, and through people seeing our marriage and family (and requesting to join it), I have realized that what we have is indeed special. I have endeavored to give some of the heart of that in these pages, although I realize that I have just begun to scratch the surface on that subject. (I may have another project to work on . . . .)

I have enjoyed searching through my picture files, looking for great quotes, and putting together this book for your learning, growth, and enjoyment. My prayer is that it will be meaningful for your life and give you great joy and encouragement to face life's challenges, and that you will make significant steps forward to reclaim who you really are. If I can ever be of service, please allow me to. It would be a blessing to my life.

God bless you all abundantly!

In Christ,
Jacqui Biernat

Printed in the USA
CPSIA information can be obtained
at www.ICGtesting.com
JSHW012013140824
68134JS00024B/2392